Introduction

Presenting Poetry provides the basis of a number of poetry sessions for primary classes (approximately 8- to 12-year-olds). The units contain:

1. a group of poems linked by a common theme, structure or feature;
2. some questions about the poems, designed to help pupils get the most out of their reading;
3. one or more follow-up activities, for example art or craft work, drama, discussion, music, recitation, choral presentation or poetry writing. These activities are often non-written and intended to show poetry as linked to the aesthetic and expressive arts.

A typical poetry session might take the following shape:

1. re-reading together of a poem or poems enjoyed in a previous session;
2. time for pupils to choose and read for pleasure, with the group, some of their favourite poems;
3. a detailed look at one unit, and follow-up work related to it. The book can, of course, also be used more informally in odd moments as a poetry anthology.

Reading the poems

When pupils meet each poem for the first time, it should be through the teacher's reading, because a well-read rendering maximises the listener's pleasure. It is strongly recommended, therefore, that teachers *practise* each poem before reading it aloud for the first time to the class. Later on, the pupils should have an opportunity to read aloud themselves. If the teacher has provided a good example of how to handle rhythm, rhyme, dramatic effects, etc., the pupil's task will be easier and more pleasurable. The pupil will also have been introduced to new or difficult words or ideas.

After this first teacher-reading of the poem, the pupil's understanding should be ensured through discussion based on the comprehension questions in the text. A second teacher-reading of the poem is often a good idea, before handing over to pupil-readers.

Although comprehension questions are included, full comprehension by all pupils of all poems is not always possible – nor is it essential. Children are well used to coping with half-grasped ideas, and may

enjoy the sounds and images of the more difficult poems for their own sake.

It is recommended that all pupil-readers be volunteers and that no pupil be forced to read. It is best to choose competent volunteers first and less competent ones later on when they have had a chance to become more familiar with words and rhythms from several hearings. It is worth trying a wide range of reading methods: single voice reading, paired reading, group reading, choral reading, and combinations of these. Happy chanting (where appropriate) is not to be despised: it gives pleasure and helps commit poems to memory. When possible and practical, children may be encouraged to use sound effects, music, etc., to accompany their readings.

Follow-up

Any follow-up work should be varied and pleasurable. Some poetry writing is included as part of a balanced follow-up programme. Unit poems are often used as a model for the pupil's work, since this is an effective way of starting children off on their own poetry writing. Learning poetry by heart is a useful memory-training exercise and can provide great pleasure. Children should be encouraged to learn their favourite poems by heart every now and then. Often poems are picked up effortlessly if they are read aloud frequently. The prospect of an audience motivates children's performance enormously. Try to provide an audience – another class, the school – for their presentations.

Contents

PRESENTING
POETRY 2

PATRICIA McCALL, SUE PALMER
AND GORDON JARVIE

Hodder & Stoughton
A MEMBER OF THE HODDER HEADLINE GROUP

Illustrations by Ian Andrew, Shirley Bellwood, Linda Birch, Francis Blake, Margaret Chamberlain, Rowan Clifford, John Fardell, Sheila Galbraith, John Harrold, Thelma Lambert, John Marshall, Steve Smallman and Guy Smith

First edition published 1986 by Oliver & Boyd

British Library Cataloguing in Publication Data
A catalogue record for this title is available from The British Library

ISBN 0 340 67006 1

First published 1986 by Oliver & Boyd
Revised edition 1996 Hodder & Stoughton
Impression number   10 9 8 7 6 5 4 3 2 1
Year   1999 1988 1997 1996

Copyright © 1996 Hodder & Stoughton

Typeset by Hewer Text Composition Services, Edinburgh.
Printed in Hong Kong for Hodder & Stoughton Educational, a division of Hodder Headline Plc, 338 Euston Road, London NW1 3BH by Colorcraft Ltd, Hong Kong.

UNIT ONE

Skool

First Day at School

A millionbillionwillion miles from home
Waiting for the bell to go. (To go where?)
Why are they all so big, other children?
So noisy? So much at home they
Must have been born in uniform
Lived all their lives in playgrounds
Spent the years inventing games
That don't let me in. Games
That are rough, that swallow you up.

And the railings.
All around, the railings.
Are they to keep out wolves and monsters?
Things that carry off and eat children?
Things you don't take sweets from?
Perhaps they're to stop us getting out
Running away from the lessins. Lessin.
What does a lessin look like?
Sounds small and slimy.
They keep them in glassrooms.
Whole rooms made out of glass. Imagine.

I wish I could remember my name.
Mummy said it would come in useful,
Like wellies. When there's puddles.
Yellowwellies. I wish she was here.
I think my name is sewn on somewhere
Perhaps the teacher will read it for me.
Tea-cher. The one who makes the tea.

Roger McGough

This little child has got a lot of things wrong about school. Find as many things as you can that he or she has misunderstood. Let a few people try reading the poem in the right kind of voice.
What do you remember about your first day at school? Do teachers make the tea? What else do they do all day?

The next little poem was made up by American school-children:

Teacher, teacher, don't be dumb,
Give me back my bubble gum!

Teacher, teacher, I declare,
Tarzan lost his underwear!

Teacher, teacher, don't be mean,
Give me a dime for the coke machine!

Do you know any other school poems like that one?

Here is a poem about one of the subjects you study at school–
arithmetic. What is arithmetic?

from ARITHMETIC

Arithmetic is where numbers fly like pigeons in and out of your head.
Arithmetic tells you how many you lose or win if you know how many
   you had before you lost or won.
Arithmetic is seven eleven all good children go to heaven – or
   five six bundle of sticks.
Arithmetic is numbers you squeeze from your head to your hand to your
   pencil to your paper till you get the answer.
Arithmetic is where the answer is right and everything is nice and you can
   look out of the window and see the blue sky – or the answer is wrong and
   you have to start all over again and try again and see if it comes out this
   time.
If you take a number and double it and double it again and then double it a
   few more times, the number gets bigger and bigger and goes higher and
   higher and only arithmetic can tell you what the number is when you decide
   to quit doubling.
Arithmetic is where you have to multiply – and you carry the multiplication
   table in your head and hope you won't lose it . . .
If you ask your mother for one fried egg for breakfast and she gives you two
   fried eggs and you eat both of them, who is better in arithmetic, you or
   your mother?

Carl Sandburg

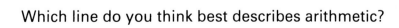

Which line do you think best describes arithmetic?

At the end of the day the bell rings and school is over:

Out of School

Four o'clock strikes,
There's a rising hum,
Then the doors fly open,
The children come.

With a wild cat-call
And a hop-scotch hop
And a bouncing ball
And a whirling top,

Grazing of knees,
A hair-pull and a slap,
A hitched-up satchel,
A pulled-down cap,

Bully boys reeling off,
Hurt ones squealing off,
Aviators wheeling off,
Mousy ones stealing off,

Woollen gloves for chilblains
Cotton rags for snufflers,
Pigtails, coat-tails,
Tails of mufflers,

Machine gun cries,
A kennelful of snarlings,
A hurricane of leaves,
A treeful of starlings,

Thinning away now
By some and some,
Thinning away, away,
All gone home.

Hal Summers

What does "aviators wheeling off" mean?
There are lots of different sounds mentioned in this poem.
Find as many as you can.
Try a class presentation of the poem. You will need seven readers, one for each stanza. They should try to follow on from each other without any breaks in the reading.
Other members of the class can be chosen to make the sounds in the background.

ACTIVITY: **Designing the Perfect School**

Try to imagine your perfect school. What sort of things would it have? What wouldn't it have?
What special rooms would there be in the perfect school?
What would the playground be like?
Work alone or with a partner.
On a large piece of paper draw a plan of your perfect school.
A plan is a bird's eye view (seen from above). You should label each room and label any special equipment you show in it.
If you have time, try working out a timetable for one day in your perfect school.

Four Fat Friars Fishing for Frogs

All the poems in this unit are examples of poets using sound to get a special effect. Poets often pick one or more letters of the alphabet and use them over and over again to make a pleasing sound for the listener.
This is called *alliteration*.

One Old Ox

One old ox opening oysters,
Two toads totally tired
Trying to trot to Tewkesbury,
Three tame tigers taking tea,
Four fat friars fishing for frogs,
Five fairies finding fire-flies,
Six soldiers shooting snipe,
Seven salmon sailing in the Solway,
Eight elegant engineers eating excellent eggs;
Nine nimble noblemen nibbling nectarines,
Ten tall tinkers tasting tamarinds,
Eleven electors eating early endive,
Twelve tremendous tale-bearers telling truth.

Anon.

Do you enjoy listening to alliteration? Why or why not?

Jargon

Jerusalem, Joppa, Jericho—
These are the cities of long ago.

Jasper, jacinth, jet and jade—
Of such are jewels for ladies made.

Juniper's green and jasmine's white,
Sweet jonquil is spring's delight.

Joseph, Jeremy, Jennifer, James,
Julian, Juliet—just names.

January, July and June—
Birthday late or birthday soon.

Jacket, jersey, jerkin, jeans—
What's the wear for sweet sixteens?

Jaguar, jackal, jumbo, jay—
Came to dinner but couldn't stay.

Jellies, junkets, jumbals, jam—
Mix them up for sweet-toothed Sam.

To jig, to jaunt, to jostle, to jest—
These are the things that Jack loves best.

Jazz, jamboree, jubilee, joke—
The jolliest words you ever spoke.

From A to Z and Z to A
The joyfullest letter of all is J.

James Reeves

Why do you think the poet chose the letter *J*
to write about?

In the next poem, the poet chooses and
repeats a sound which matches his subject.
This poem is fun to read aloud.

The Supermarket Serpent

Excuzzzzze me missus
I'm the ssupermarket sserpent
I ssslither around the sssoup and the
sssspaghetti ssectionsssss.
Sssstout Mrsssss Sssimonsssss
hearsss a hissss
but ssseesssssss nozzzzing
ssso I sslitherss up and sswallowss her
sssssssssssssssssssssssssssssssssssssssss.

Andrew Davies

9

The last poem in this unit is by an eleven-year-old boy. Donald's teacher told him about alliteration and now he finds it very useful when writing poetry of his own.

Count Dracula

Beware dangerous Dracula during dusk,
With fiendish fangs for finely finding flesh.
Dracula has electric eyes:
Even the werewolves don't dare disobey the terrible count.

Dracula disappears into a beastly black bat,
To deal deadly with delicious necks.
He stands many mighty metres high,
And wears a black and blood-red capacious cloak
Capable of hiding him horribly.
He lives in a creepy castle, certainly empty—
His castle is in terrible Transylvania,
Though not many vexed victims go there.

Donald Finlay

ACTIVITY I: Poetry Writing

Choose one of the following:
1. Use *One Old Ox* as a model and write a similar poem.
2. Use alliteration to write the most fiendish tongue-twister you can.
3. Try a snake poem of your own, using lots of *s* sounds.

Your poem need not rhyme, but remember to begin each new line with a capital letter.

ACTIVITY 2: Alliteration Collage

Newspaper headlines and advertisements often make use of alliteration. It catches the reader's eye and keeps the message in the reader's memory.
Make a collage of alliteration cuttings from newspapers and magazines.

When the Lights Go Out

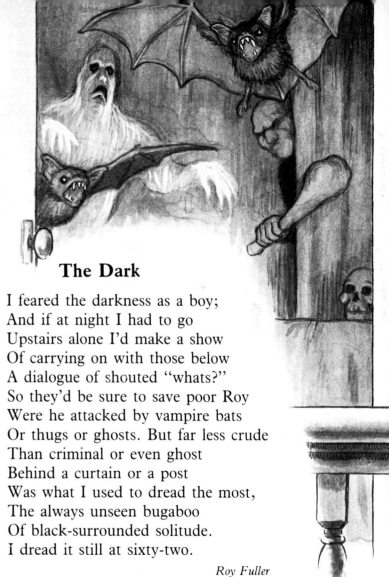

The Dark

I feared the darkness as a boy;
And if at night I had to go
Upstairs alone I'd make a show
Of carrying on with those below
A dialogue of shouted "whats?"
So they'd be sure to save poor Roy
Were he attacked by vampire bats
Or thugs or ghosts. But far less crude
Than criminal or even ghost
Behind a curtain or a post
Was what I used to dread the most,
The always unseen bugaboo
Of black-surrounded solitude.
I dread it still at sixty-two.

Roy Fuller

What does the poet mean by *black-surrounded solitude* (second last line)?

11

The Longest Journey in the World

'Last one into bed
has to switch out the light.'
It's just the same every night.
There's a race.
I'm ripping off my trousers and shirt,
he's kicking of his shoes and socks.

'My sleeve's stuck.
This button's too big for its button-hole.'
Have you hidden my pyjamas?
Keep your hands off mine.

If you win
you get where it's safe
before the darkness comes
but if you lose
if you're last
you know what you've got coming up is
The Longest Journey in The World.

There is nowhere so dark
as that room in the moment
after I've switched out the light.
There is nowhere so full of dangerous things.
Things that love dark places.
Things that breathe only when you breathe
and hold their breath when I hold mine.

So I have to say:
'I'm not scared.'
That face, grinning in the pattern on the wall
Isn't a face—
'I'm not scared.'
That prickle on the back of my neck
is only the label on my pyjama jacket—
'I'm not scared.'
That moaning-moaning is nothing
but water in a pipe—
'I'm not scared.'

Everything's going to be just fine
as soon as I get into that bed of mine.
Such a terrible shame
It's always the same
It takes so long
it takes so long
it takes so long
to make it there.

Michael Rosen

Are you afraid of the dark? What is it that is so
frightening?
Do the same things scare you now that scared
you when you were younger?
Do you think you will *dread it still at sixty-two*?
Is it silly to be afraid of the dark?
Is it sensible to be afraid of the dark?

Whatif

Last night, while I lay thinking here,
Some Whatifs crawled inside my ear
And pranced and partied all night long
And sang their same old Whatif song:
Whatif I'm dumb in school?
Whatif they've closed the swimming pool?
Whatif I get beat up?
Whatif there's poison in my cup?
Whatif I start to cry?
Whatif I get sick and die?
Whatif I flunk that test?
Whatif green hair grows on my chest?
Whatif nobody likes me?
Whatif a bolt of lightning strikes me?
Whatif I don't grow taller?
Whatif my head starts getting smaller?
Whatif the fish won't bite?
Whatif the wind tears up my kite?
Whatif they start a war?
Whatif my parents get divorced?
Whatif the bus is late?
Whatif my teeth don't grow in straight?
Whatif I tear my pants?
Whatif I never learn to dance?
Everything seems swell, and then
The nighttime Whatifs strike again!

Shel Silverstein

What are the Whatifs that worry you?
What is the worst Whatif in the poem?
Try asking some of the adults that you know
what frightens them more – the dark or the
Whatifs?

ACTIVITY: **Whatif Frieze**

There is an illustration of Whatifs near the
poem. This is how the artist imagined them.
Which ones are they? What might some of the
other Whatifs look like? Try a class frieze of
Whatifs attacking a child. A good way to begin it
is to draw a life-size figure (get a member of the
class to lie down on a big piece of paper while
someone draws round him/her). Everyone could
then draw or paint a Whatif to cut out and glue
on the frieze. It could be one from the poem or a
Whatif that worries you.

Shel Silverstein

Shel Silverstein, who wrote the *Whatif* poem in the last unit, is a modern American poet. He was born in Chicago, Illinois. As well as writing poems, he also writes songs and draws cartoons. Most of his poems are funny and very enjoyable. If you like Shel Silverstein's poems, you may want to read more of his work. He has published several books of poems including *Where The Sidewalk Ends* and *A Light In The Attic*. You may be able to request these from your school or public library.

What sort of animals do you think might live in a cooker, a washing machine or a hoover? How might you know they were there?

Bear in There

There's a Polar Bear
In our Frigidaire—
He likes it 'cause it's cold in there.
With his seat in the meat
And his face in the fish
And his big hairy paws
In the buttery dish,
He's nibbling the noodles,
He's munching the rice,
He's slurping the soda,
He's licking the ice.
And he lets out a roar
If you open the door.

And it gives me a scare
To know he's in there—
That Polary Bear
In our Fridgitydaire.

Shel Silverstein

Little Abigail and the Beautiful Pony

There was a girl named Abigail
Who was taking a ride
Through the country
With her parents
When she spied a beautiful sad-eyed
Grey and white pony
And next to it was a sign
That said,
FOR SALE—CHEAP.
"Oh," said Abigail,
"May I have that pony?
May I please?"
And her parents said,
"No you may not."
And Abigail said,
"But I MUST have that pony."
And her parents said,
"Well, you can't have that pony,
But you can have a nice butter pecan
Ice cream cone when we get home."

And Abigail said,
"I don't want a butter pecan
Ice cream cone,
I WANT THAT PONY—
I MUST HAVE THAT PONY."
And her parents said,
"Be quiet and stop nagging—
You're *not* getting that pony."
And Abigail began to cry and said,
"If I don't get that pony I'll die."

And her parents said, "You won't die.
No child ever died yet from not getting a pony."
And Abigail felt so bad
That when they got home she went to bed,
And she couldn't eat,
And she couldn't sleep,
And her heart was broken,
And she DID die—
All because of a pony
That her parents wouldn't buy.

(This is a good story
To read to your folks
When they won't buy
You something you want.)

Shel Silverstein

THE PONY
THAT THEY
WOULDN'T
BUY ME.
.TOO LATE!

Try finding the right voices to use for every part of this poem. Practise reading it aloud. You might want to work in groups of four: one narrator, one Abigail, and two parents speaking together.

The Silver Fish

While fishing in the blue lagoon,
I caught a lovely silver fish,
And he spoke to me, "My boy," quoth he,
"Please set me free and I'll grant your wish;
A kingdom of wisdom? A palace of gold?
Or all the fancies your mind can hold?"
And I said, "O.K.", and I set him free,
But he laughed at me as he swam away,
And left me whispering my wish
Into a silent sea.

Today I caught that fish again
(That lovely silver prince of fishes),
And once again he offered me,
If I would only set him free,
Any one of a number of wishes
If I would throw him back to the fishes.

He was delicious.

Shel Silverstein

What would you say the moral of that tale was?

The next poem is really a "Knock Knock" joke.

The Meehoo with an Exactlywatt

Knock knock!
    Who's there?
Me!
    Me who?
That's right!
    What's right?
Meehoo!
    That's what I want to know!
What's what you want to know?
    Me who?
Yes, exactly!
    Exactly *what?*
Yes, I have an Exactlywatt on a chain!
    Exactly *what* on a chain?
Yes!
    Yes *what?*
No, Exactlywatt!
    That's what I want to know!
I told you—Exactlywatt!
    Exactly *what?*
Yes!
    Yes what?
Yes, it's with me!
    What's with you?
Exactlywatt—that's what's with me.
    Me who?
Yes!
    Go away!
Knock knock . . .

Shel Silverstein

Take turns to read this poem aloud in pairs. Although it sounds rather muddling it is quite easy to read, because whenever the Meehoo speaks the line begins further over to the left. Whenever the person behind the door speaks, the line begins further to the right.

ACTIVITY: Joke Collecting

You probably know lots of "Knock Knock" jokes and it is fun to make a collection of them.
1. Divide into groups of four to six and chat about the jokes you know.
2. Practise telling them with a partner from your group.
3. Get together a group presentation of your jokes to show the class.
4. Decide as a class which jokes are best and make a class tape of "Knock Knock" jokes.

Rhythm

Look back at page 5 and read *Teacher, Teacher* again. Can you hear its very strong rhythm? Tap out the rhythm with your fingers as your teacher reads the poem aloud. The rhythm is so strong that this poem makes a very good chant. Try chanting it together as a class.

Many people like poetry with a strong rhythm. Why do you think this is so?

Look at the unit poems you know and pick out some more poems with a strong rhythm. Read them aloud to show the rhythm. Sometimes poets use rhythm to get special effects. The rhythm of the next poem is meant to be the tramping of marching feet.

Shadow March

All around the house is the jet black night;
It stares through the window pane;
It crawls in the corners, hiding from the light,
And it moves with the moving flame.

Now my little heart goes a-beating like a drum,
With the breath of the Bogie in my hair;
And all around the candle the crooked shadows come,
And go marching along up the stair.

The shadow of the balusters, the shadow of the lamp,
The shadow of the child that goes to bed—
All the wicked shadows coming, tramp, tramp, tramp,
With the black night overhead.

Robert Louis Stevenson

Listen to your teacher read this poem a couple of times, until you can really hear the rhythm. Now some members of the class can try. Once you can read the poem very rhythmically, you may want to add some heart-beat sounds, heavy breathing and foot-tramping in the right places.

The next poem is the first verse of a long story-poem. The story is about three riders racing from one town to another with some important news. The poet has tried to make his rhythm like galloping horses.

How They Brought the Good News from Ghent to Aix

I sprang to the stirrup, and Joris, and he;
I galloped, Dirck galloped, we galloped all three;
"Good speed!" cried the watch, as the gate bolts
    undrew,
"Speed!" echoed the wall to us galloping through;
Behind shut the postern, the lights sank to rest,
And into the midnight we galloped abreast.

Robert Browning

watch – the watchman
postern – the back gate

What is happening in these few lines?
Can you hear the galloping rhythm?
Let a few people try to read it at a gallop.
It's quite hard to do.

The rhythm of the next poem is meant to be the rhythm of a train, rushing through Scotland to deliver the mail on time. (The shapes at the side are explained in the Activity section.)

Night Mail

● This is the night mail crossing the border,
   Bringing the cheque and the postal order,
■ Letters for the rich, letters for the poor,
   The shop at the corner and the girl next door.
◆ Pulling up Beattock, a steady climb—
   The gradient's against her, but she's on time.
● Past cotton grass and moorland boulder,
   Shovelling white steam over her shoulder,
■ Snorting noisily as she passes
   Silent miles of wind-bent grasses.
◆ Birds turn their heads as she approaches,
   Stare from the bushes at her black-faced coaches
● Sheep-dogs cannot turn her course,
   They slumber on with paws across.
■ In the farm she passes no one wakes,
   But a jug in the bedroom gently shakes.

✱ Dawn freshens, the climb is done.
   Down towards Glasgow she descends
   Towards the steam tugs yelping down the glade
      of cranes,
   Towards the fields of apparatus, the furnaces
   Set on the dark plain like gigantic chessmen.
   All Scotland waits for her:
   In the dark glens, beside the pale-green lochs
   Men long for news.

◆ Letters of thanks, letters from banks,
● Letters of joy from girl and boy,
■ Receipted bills and invitations
   To inspect new stock or visit relations,

19

◆ And applications for situations
● And timid lovers' declarations
→ And gossip, gossip from all the nations,
■ News circumstantial, news financial,
◆ Letters with holiday snaps to enlarge in,
● Letters with faces scrawled in the margin,
■ Letters from uncles, cousins, and aunts,
◆ Letters to Scotland from
   the South of France,
● Letters of condolence to
   Highlands and Lowlands,
Notes from overseas to Hebrides;

■ Written on paper of every hue,
◆ The pink, the violet, the white and the blue,
● The chatty, the catty, the boring, adoring,
■ The cold and official and the heart's outpouring,
◆ Clever, stupid, short and long,
→ The typed and the printed and the spelt all wrong.

✳ Thousands are still asleep
Dreaming of terrifying monsters,
Or of friendly tea beside the band at Cranston's
   or Crawford's,

● Asleep in working Glasgow, asleep
   in well-set Edinburgh,
Asleep in granite Aberdeen,
✳ They continue their dreams;
But shall wake soon and long for
   letters,
And none will hear the postman's
   knock
Without a quickening of the heart,
For who can bear to feel himself
   forgotten?

W. H. Auden

The poem is in four main sections.
The first section is marked with ●, ■, ◆. In this section the train is rushing on its way. You can hear its rhythm changing as it goes over different sorts of countryside.
What do you think Beattock is? Why?
How does the rhythm change in the two lines about Beattock? Read the first section again.

The second section is marked with a ✳. Here someone is telling the story, and we cannot hear the train's rhythm any more.

The third section tells about the sorts of letters the train carries. We can hear the train's rhythm again.

Discuss what these mean with your teacher:
    Receipted bills
    Applications for situations
    Timid lovers' declarations
    News financial
    Letters of condolence.
Read the third section again.

In the last section the story-teller finishes off the poem.

ACTIVITY I: **Choral Reading**

This poem is very good for reading in groups. The signs on the left-hand side show who reads which part. Your class should divide into three main groups plus one good reader to be the story-teller.

The groups are ●, ■, ◆. Each group reads the parts marked with its sign.
The story-teller reads the parts marked ✳.
Where you see an arrow (→), everyone should join in.
You need to practise this several times to get it right. Each group should be ready to start reading their next bit *as soon as* the group before has stopped. There should be no unwanted pauses.
Try to get the train rhythm sounding really strong in the first and third sections.
When you have practised, try to put this poem on tape for another class to hear.

ACTIVITY 2: **Letter Display**

1. Read the letter section of *Night Mail* again.
2. Choose one of the types mentioned there, and try to write that sort of letter. Talk about the letters first with your teacher – is there anything special about the way it will be written (the sort of words or mood needed for that type of letter)?
Try to make sure that someone in the class is doing an example of every type of letter mentioned in the poem.
3. You could copy your finished letters on to *paper of every hue*, as it says in the poem, and make a wall display for the classroom.

Double, Double, Toil and Trouble

From ancient times, spells and charms have been written as poems. Perhaps witches and wizards felt that poetry had more magic in it than ordinary words.

Here are two old charms which are supposed to cure the hiccups:

Hiccup, hiccup, go away,
Come again another day:
Hiccup, hiccup, when I bake,
I'll give to you a butter-cake.

Hiccup, snickup,
Rise up, right up,
Three drops in a cup
Are good for the hiccup.

Try them next time you're hiccupping and see if they work!

In a play called *Macbeth* by William Shakespeare there were three evil witches. Here is the spell they brewed in their steaming cauldron:

The Witches' Song

Double, double, toil and trouble; 1
Fire burn, and cauldron bubble.

Fillet of a fenny snake,
In the cauldron boil and bake;
Eye of newt, and toe of frog, 5
Wool of bat, and tongue of dog,
Adder's fork, and blind-worm's sting,
Lizard's leg, and howlet's wing,
For a charm of powerful trouble,
Like a hell-broth boil and bubble. 10

Double, double, toil and trouble;
Fire burn, and cauldron bubble.

William Shakespeare

fenny – from the fen (line 3)
howlet – young owl (line 8)

Do you think this spell is for something nice or nasty? Why?
Look away from the book. How many of the ingredients for Shakespeare's spell can you remember?
Try chanting the spell all together in witchy voices. Get someone to make a few mad cackles in the background!

Another charm, written about the same time, might come in useful:

Charme to Keep Witches Away

Bring the holy crust of Bread,
Lay it underneath the head;
'Tis a certain Charme to keep
Hags away, while Children Sleep.

Robert Herrick

What do you think the 'holy crust of Bread' is?

Or how about this modern spell?

Spell to Make Your Teacher Disappear

From the blackboard gather chalk-dust,
Mix it with a drop of ink,
Put it in an empty paint-pot
Rinsed out at the staff-room sink.

Stir it gently with a ruler,
Let it bubble till it's thick.
Make a pair of magic passes
O'er it with a metre stick.

Gently chant the eight times table
Backwards down to eight times one;
Leave it now to gather power—
Soon the magic will be done.

As the hometime bell is ringing
Cringe and wait in fright and fear:
Watch your teacher put her coat on . . .
Watch!—and soon she'll disappear!

S. J. Saunders

Do you think it would work?

ACTIVITY: Making Up a Spell

Look back at the sort of ingredients that go into spells. What other instructions do spells include, as well as the ingredients?
Choose something to make up a spell about. Think of the type of ingredients you might need. Think of the other instructions you could give.
Try making up a spell of your own, written like a poem. For a spell, it might be better if you can make your poem rhyme.

UNIT SEVEN

Bad Boys

Tom's Bomb

There was a boy whose name was Tom,
Who made a high explosive bomb,
By mixing up some iodine
With sugar, flour and Plasticine.
Then, to make it smell more queer,
He added Daddy's home-made beer.
He took it off to school one day,
And when they all went out to play,
He left it by the radiator.
As the heat was getting greater,
The mixture in the bomb grew thick
And very soon it seemed to tick.
Miss Knight came in and gazed with awe
To see the bomb upon the floor.
'Dear me,' she said, 'it is a bomb,
An object worth escaping from.'
She went to Mr. Holliday
And said in tones that were not gay,
'Headmaster, this is not much fun;
There is a bomb in Classroom One.'
'Great snakes,' he said, and gave a cough
And said, 'I hope it won't go off.
But on the off-chance that it does,
I think we'd better call the fuzz.'
A policeman came and said, 'Oh God,
We need the bomb disposal squad,
Some firemen and a doctor too,

A helicopter and its crew,
And, since I'm shaking in the legs,
A pot of tea and hard-boiled eggs.'
A bomb disposal engineer
Said, with every sign of fear,
'I've not seen one like that before,'
And rushed out, screaming, through the door.
Everyone became more worried
Till Tom, who seemed to be unflurried,
Asked what was all the fuss about?
'I'll pick it up and take it out.'
He tipped the contents down the drain
And peace and quiet reigned again.
Tom just smiled and shook his head
And quietly to himself he said:
'Excitement's what these people seek.
I'll bring another one next week.'

David Hornsby

Do you think Tom's bomb would really have gone off?

In the next poem the bad boy tells his own story. Read it to yourself first. Then some people could try saying it in the right kind of voice.

Nooligan

I'm a nooligan
don't give a toss
in our class
I'm the boss
(well, one of them)

I'm a nooligan
got a nard 'ead
step out of line
and you're dead
(well, bleedin)

I'm a nooligan
I spray me name
all over town
footballs me game
(well, watchin)

I'm a nooligan
violence is fun
gonna be a nassassin
or a hired gun
(well, a soldier)

Roger McGough

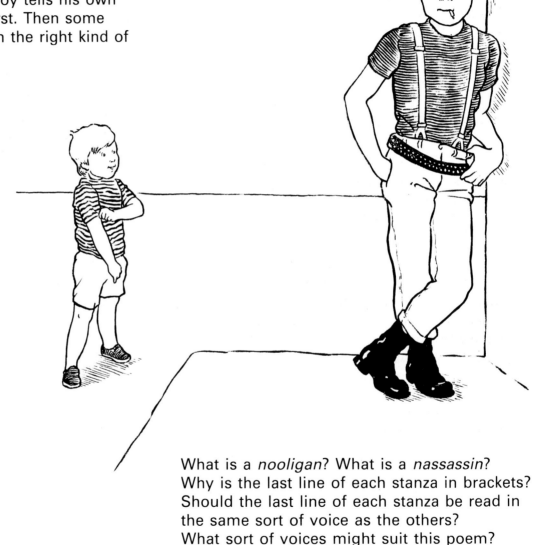

What is a *nooligan*? What is a *nassassin*?
Why is the last line of each stanza in brackets?
Should the last line of each stanza be read in the same sort of voice as the others?
What sort of voices might suit this poem?

Little Johnny's Confession

This morning
    being rather young and foolish
    I borrowed a machine-gun my father
    had left hidden since the war, went out,
    and eliminated a number of small enemies.
    Since then I have not returned home.

This morning
    swarms of police with trackerdogs
    wander about the city
    with my description printed
    on their minds, asking:
    'Have you seen him?
    He is seven years old,
    likes Pluto, Mighty Mouse
    and Biffo the Bear,
    have you seen him, anywhere?'

This morning
    sitting alone in a strange playground
    muttering you've blundered, you've blundered
    over and over to myself
    I work out my next move
    but cannot move.
    The trackerdogs will sniff me out,
    they have my lollypops.

Brian Patten

What sort of voice might be suitable for this poem?
Which of these poems do you think is the most true to life? Why?
Which do you think is least likely? Why?

ACTIVITY: Wanted Posters

Here is an artist's idea of a *WANTED* poster the police might have made for Little Johnny. Imagine that you have been bad, and design a *WANTED* poster for yourself! Think up something wicked you might have done, make up a good description of yourself (as funny as you can), and add a picture.

Man's Best Friend

Choosing a Friend

'Bring an old towel,' said Pa,
'And a scrap of meat from the pantry.
We're going out in the car, you and I,
Into the country.'

I did as he asked, although
I couldn't see why he wanted
An old towel and a scrap of meat.
Into the sun we pointed

Our Ford, over the green hills.
Pa sang. Larks bubbled in the sky.
I'd brought with me all my cards—
It was my seventh birthday.

We turned down a happy lane,
Half sunlight, half shadow,
And saw at the end a white house
In a yellow meadow.

Mrs Garner lived there. She was tall.
She gave me a glass of milk
And showed me her black spaniel.
'Her name is Silk,'

Mrs Garner said, 'She's got
Three puppies, two black, one golden.
Come and see them.' Oh,
To have one, one of my own!

'You can choose one,' said Pa.
I looked at him. He wasn't joking.
I could scarcely say Thank you.
I was almost choking.

It was the golden one. He slept
On my knee in the old towel
All the way home. He was tiny,
But he didn't whimper or howl,

Not once. That was a year ago,
And now I'm eight.
When I get home from school
He'll be waiting behind the gate,

Listening, listening hard,
Head raised, eyes warm and kind.
He came to me as a gift
And grew into a friend.

Leslie Norris

Which puppy would you have
chosen? What would you have
called it?

28

The boy in the poem looks at his father when he offers him the puppy because he isn't sure whether or not his father is joking. Can you always tell when adults are joking?

In what ways can a pet dog be a friend? How do dogs help people?

Once you have heard your teacher reading this poem, some members of the class might like to try it. Be careful of the parts (stanzas 2–3 and 8–9) where sentences cross over from one stanza to another. Three people could read – one to be the child, one to be Pa and one to be Mrs Garner.

Here is a poem about a dog who is very different:

What do you imagine the lone dog looks like? Do you think he is happy? Why or why not? In what ways is the lone dog different from the dog in *Choosing A Friend*? What sort of reading voice do you think would suit this poem?

Lone Dog

I'm a lean dog, a keen dog, a wild dog and lone.
I'm a rough dog, a tough dog, hunting on my own!
I'm a bad dog, a mad dog, teasing silly sheep;
I love to sit and bay the moon and keep fat souls from sleep.

I'll never be a lap dog, licking dirty feet,
A sleek dog, a meek dog, cringing for my meat.
Not for me the fireside, the well-filled plate,
But shut door and sharp stone and cuff and kick and hate.

Not for me the other dogs, running by my side,
Some have run a short while, but none of them would bide.
O mine is the lone trail, the hard trail, the best,
Wide wind and wild stars and the hunger of the quest.

Irene McLeod

The last poem is about a dog long ago. He belonged to a Greek adventurer called Ulysses, who went away to fight in a war at a place called Troy. You may have heard about Ulysses' story. It was twenty years before he returned home, and he had many adventures on the way. His dog, Argus, waited for him all that time.

Argus and Ulysses

Argus was a puppy
Frisking full of joy.
Ulysses was his master
Who sailed away to Troy.

Argus on the seashore
Watched the ship's white track,
And barked a little puppy-bark
To bring his master back.

Argus was an old dog,
Too grey and tired for tears.
He lay outside the house-door
And watched for twenty years.

When twenty years were ended
Ulysses came from Troy.
Argus wagged an old dog's wag
And then he died for joy.

Eleanor Farjeon

Argus remembered Ulysses for twenty years. Do the dogs you know remember people they haven't seen for a long time? What about other animals?
Do you know any other stories about the faithfulness of animals?

ACTIVITY: An Anthology of Cat Poems

There are not many poems about dogs, but there are hundreds about cats. Poets seem to like writing about cats. Try making a class anthology of cat poems. An anthology is a collection of writing. Try making a class anthology of cat poems. An anthology is a collection of writing.

You will need to look through lots of poetry books. There may be some other poetry books in the classroom or school library? You could borrow some from other teachers (but remember to write each teacher's name inside each book in pencil, to make returning easy). Poetry books could also be brought from home or the public library.

Find as many cat poems as you can, and write them out neatly on paper. You can mount these into a book of coloured pages and decorate it with pictures of cats.

Bairn Rhymes

James King Annand (1908-1993) was an Edinburgh schoolmaster, and his children's poetry is often short and snappy and funny. Many of these "bairn rhymes" – as he called them – are about particular birds and animals, or about people and their work. You'll see that Annand wrote in his native Scots tongue rather than in Standard English, and a few Scots words are explained after the poems in case you don't recognise them.

Do you think it is a good idea to write in Scots rather than in Standard English? Why/why not?

Another Scots writer of bairn rhymes was William Soutar (1898-1943). You might like to look for some of his work.

Robin Reidbriest

Robin, Robin Reidbreist,
Happin on a brier
Oot amang the snaw and ice,
While I sit by the fire.
Tell me in your bonnie sang
That ye're my frien sae true,
And I shall gie ye meat and drink
The hail winter throu.

Houlet

The houlet has the whoopin cough,
Whoop, whoop, whoopin!
Whoopin up and whoopin doun,
Whoopin throu the ferm toun,
Wauknin ilka lass and loun,
Whoop, whoop, whoopin.
Houlet wi the whoopin cough,
Whoop, whoop, whoopin,
Dae your whoopin by and by!
Be like ither birds and try
To haud your wheest and let me lie
Sleep, sleep, sleepin.

Water-craw

Water-craw, Water-craw,
Coat o black
And vest like snaw.
Bob to left,
Bob to richt,
Gie your dirty neb a dicht.
Bob again and flee awa
To seek your supper,
Water-craw.

happin: hopping
hail: whole
houlet: owl
wauknin: wakening
ilka: every
loun: boy
haud your wheest: hold your peace, keep quiet
water-craw: water wagtail
dicht: wipe

Come Sailin

Come intil my boat
I'll tak ye for a sail,
We'll mebbe catch a cod,
A mackerel or a whale,
We'll mebbe catch a mermaid
And we will be enthralled.
But I think it far mair likely
We'll only catch the cauld.

Zebra

In winter time when it was dark
A pownie gaed to Hampden Park.
His coat was wearin thin and auld,
Nae wunder he was feelin cauld.

He saw some washin on the line
And shouted, "This will dae me fine."
He streekit owre his heid and back
A jersey strippit white and black
And lookin like a fitba player
Lowpt like a rocket through the air,
And when he landit back frae Space
Foundit the African zebra race.

gaed: went   *lowpt*: leapt
streekit: stretched

Rain

Rain-draps, rain-draps,
Stottin aff stanes,
Grannie tellt us ye wad come,
She felt it in her banes.

Rain-draps, rain-draps,
Skytin aff sclates,
Getherin in your millions till
The burns rowe doun in spates.

Rain-draps, rain-draps,
Batterin on the pane,
Bash yersels to smithereens
And dinna come again.

skytin: bouncing   *rowe*: rush

Cup o Tea

My Mither yaises tea-bags
To mask a pot o tea.
They dinna make a slaister
When pourin out the bree.

But Grannie yaises tea-leafs when
She entertains a frien'.
She keeps them in a caddy wi
A likeness o the Queen.

And aye afore she pours your tea
She'll steer the tea-leafs up
– She canna spae your fortune wi
Nae tea-leafs in your cup.

yaises: uses   *bree*: dregs
mask: infuse   *spae*: guess
slaister: mess

Space Honeymoon

I'm gaun to mairry
The Man-in-the-Mune
At hauf-past-three
This eftirnune.
We've spoken for a sputnik
Wrocht by solar ray
To tak us on our honeymoon
Alang the Milky Way.

wrocht: powered   *spoken for*: ordered

Donkey Ride

The day we had a picnic
Aside the Firth o Clyde
I hired mysel a cuddy
To tak me for a ride.

I said, "Gee-up my cuddy!"
I slapped him wi my hand.
The cuddy loutit doun
And cowpt me on the sand.

Ye can keep you cuddy,
Ye can keep your ride,
I'm stickin to the motor
Wi Daddy by my side.

loutit: knelt   *cowpt*: dumped

Fishin Boat

Jings I'm wishin
They'd tak me to the fishin.
Gif I catcht a haddie
I'd fry it for my daddy.
Gif I catcht anither
I'd cook it for my mither.
Gif I catcht three
We'd aa hae fish for tea.

Grumphie

Grumphie, Grumphie,
Howkin in the midden,
Daein what ye like,
Never as ye're bidden.

Grumphie, Grumphie,
Slorpin up your meat,
Sic a slaister
When ye eat.

Grumphie, Grumphie,
Snorin in your sty,
Ye'll be bacon
Bye and bye.

grumphie: pig *sic*: such
howkin: poking *slaister*: mess

Hielant Games

I entered for the Hielant Games
But couldna rin for toffee,
I tummelt in the lowpin-pit,
My caber toss was awfu'!

I wish I were a mountain hare –
I'd be the fastest sprinter there.

I wish I were a kangaroo –
I'd lowp frae here to Timbuctoo.

I wish I were an Ayrshire bull –
I'd toss them to the Isle of Mull.

Gif I'd the talent o the three,
Sic a Champion I wad be!

tummelt: tumbled *sic*: such *gif*: if

Cat and Mous

Said the poussie
Til the mousie,
"Let me intil
Your wee housie.
We will play
And we will sing
And we will dance
A jingo-ring."

Said the mousie
Til the poussie,
"Ye'll no get
In my wee housie.

Ye are big
And I am wee
And ye wad eat me
For your tea."

wad: would

34

Guddlin

Guddlin in the burn
Sandy fand a troot,
Grupp't it by the gills
And smertly flang it oot.

He didna need a worm,
He didna need a flie,
Bit soopleness o haun
And glegness in his ee.

He built a bonnie fire
To roast his caller fish–
It aye tastes better stickit
Nor servit in a dish.

fand: found	*glegness*: quickness
flang: flung	*ee*: eye
haun: hand	*caller*: fresh

A Finger Game

Five wee birdies sittin on a dyke.
Ane gaed to Penicuik to buy a motor bike.

Fower wee birdies sittin in a raw.
Ane flew to Jeddart Toun to see the Hand-baa.

Three wee birdies sittin in a line.
Twa sat on and ane gaed to dine.

Twa wee birdies sittin on a stane.
Ane took the huff and then there was ane.

Ane wee birdie sittin aa his lane.
Gangs awa at bedtime and nou there are nane.

ACTIVITY 1: Recitation
Each try and learn one of Annand's bairn rhymes around the class as a party piece. Practise saying it until you're happy with it and think you've got it just about right. Then the class can recite the poems to another class. Let the other class judge who are the best reciters.
Now you've got a stand-by recitation for Halloween or for family get-togethers.

ACTIVITY 2: Writing
On your own or in pairs, try writing one or two of your own bairn rhymes. Choose simple, everyday subjects – a sparrow, a tadpole, the postman – and see if you can write something amusing about them. Read your poems to the class.

UNIT TEN

Riddles

Some of the earliest poems we know of are riddles. The poet describes a common thing in an unusual way and you have to guess what it is.

Can you guess what these are?

1. In Spring I look gay
   Decked in comely array,
   In Summer more clothing I wear;
   When colder it grows
   I fling off my clothes
   And in Winter quite naked appear.

2. In marble walls as white as milk,
   Lined with a skin as soft as silk,
   Within a fountain crystal clear
   A golden apple doth appear;
   No doors there are to this stronghold
   Yet thieves break in and steal the gold.

The answers are on page 48.

This old riddle seems very odd to begin with, but it's quite funny when you know the answer:

3. Four stiff standers,
   Four dilly-danders,
   Two lookers,
   Two crookers,
   And a wig-wag.

Clue: It's an animal.   Answer on page 48.

M. C. Escher: Metamorphosis – a picture riddle

The last riddle is the oldest of all. It was written over a thousand years ago in Anglo-Saxon, the language used in England before modern English developed. It has been translated by Michael Alexander.

4. I am clad in red, a rich man's treasure.
   I was a steep hard place: plants grew on me,
   Bright to look at. What's left of me now
   Is the work of the fire, the file's anger:
   Tightly imprisoned; made precious with wire.
   One who wears gold may weep at my bite
   When I dash to pieces his precious treasure.

Answer on page 48.

Read all the riddles through again now that you know the answers. Which do you think is best? Why?
What tricks do the poets use when they are describing things in their riddles, so that you will not know what they are?

Answer on page 48.

ACTIVITY: **Riddle Competition**

Choose something that people see every day. Write a short poem describing it, but don't say what it is. Try to make it difficult to guess. Your poem does not have to rhyme, but you should start each new thought on a new line. And each line should begin with a capital letter.
It is fun to make a flash card of your riddle. Copy the riddle poem neatly on one side of a card. On the other side draw a picture of the answer. When everyone has finished their riddles, you could have a competition to guess the answers, using your flash cards.

Going, Going, Gone . . .

The Dodo

The Dodo used to walk around
And take the sun and air.
The sun yet warms his native ground—
The Dodo is not there!

The voice which used to squawk and squeak
Is now forever dumb—
Yet you may see his bones and beak
All in the museum.

Hilaire Belloc

This poem is funny, but the story of the poor dodo is not very funny at all. The dodo was a bird which used to live on the island of Mauritius in the Indian Ocean. This island was often used by sailors as a place to stop and get water. The dodo was not used to people and would sit still while they approached. The sailors clubbed many of the poor dodos to death for food. Others were killed by pigs released on to the island. Eventually the species became extinct.

Why is the extinction of an animal species such a dreadful thing? Sometimes Nature causes a species to become extinct, as in the case of the dinosaurs. Sometimes people cause it to happen, as in the case of the dodo. Which is worse, and why?

The next poem is about the buffalo which used to roam the plains of North America in vast herds, providing food and clothing for the Plains Indians. As the white settlers moved across America in the long struggle to win the West, they shot millions of buffaloes for sport. They also deliberately shot them to remove the food supply of the Indians.

Is the buffalo extinct? What does the poet mean when he says *the buffaloes are gone*? Who were *those who saw the buffaloes* and what happened to them?

Buffalo Dusk

The buffaloes are gone.
And those who saw the buffaloes are gone.
Those who saw the buffaloes by thousands and
   how they pawed the prairie sod into dust
   with their hoofs, their great heads down
   pawing on in a great pageant of dusk,
Those who saw the buffaloes are gone.
And the buffaloes are gone.

Carl Sandburg

To See the Rabbit

WE are going to see the rabbit.
We are going to see the rabbit.
Which rabbit, people say?
Which rabbit, ask the children?
Which rabbit?
The only rabbit,
The only rabbit in England,
Sitting behind a barbed-wire fence
Under the floodlights, neon lights,
Sodium lights,
Nibbling grass
On the only patch of grass
In England, in England
(Except the grass by the hoardings
Which doesn't count).
We are going to see the rabbit
And we must be there on time.

First we shall go by escalator,
Then we shall go by underground,
And then we shall go by motorway,
And then by helicopterway,
And the last ten yards we shall have to go
On foot.

And now we are going
All the way to see the rabbit,
We are nearly there,
We are longing to see it,
And so is the crowd

Which is here in thousands
With mounted policemen
And big loudspeakers
And bands and banners,
And everyone has come a long way.

But soon we shall see it
Sitting and nibbling
The blades of grass
On the only patch of grass
In—but something has gone wrong!
Why is everyone so angry,
Why is everyone jostling
And slanging and complaining?

The rabbit has gone,
Yes, the rabbit has gone.
He has actually burrowed down into the earth
And made himself a warren, under the earth,
Despite all these people,
And what shall we do?
What *can* we do?

It is all a pity, you must be disappointed,
Go home and do something else for today,
Go home again, go home for today.
For you cannot hear the rabbit, under the earth,
Remarking rather sadly to himself, by himself,
As he rests in his warren, under the earth:
'It won't be long, they are bound to come,
They are bound to come and find me, even here.'

Alan Brownjohn

When does this poem take place? How do you know?
What sort of world does the poet paint a picture of?
What has happened to all the rabbits and why?
Could this really happen?

ACTIVITY: **Choral Presentation of**
To See the Rabbit

1. Divide up into groups of about four to six.
2. Talk about the best way to read the poem aloud. Who should say what? Do you need a narrator? Would some parts be best read by several of you together? What sort of voices will you need to use? Can you add any sound effects to your reading?
3. Practise until your group has a good presentation.
4. Tape your presentation or perform it for the rest of the class. Try to show another class what you have done.

UNIT TWELVE

In the Beginning

The first poem in this unit is an extract from the Bible. It is from *Genesis*, the first book of the Old Testament.

In the beginning God created 1
the heaven and the earth.
  And the earth was without form,
and void; and darkness was upon
the face of the deep. And the Spirit 5
of God moved upon the face of
the waters.
  And God said, Let there be
light: and there was light.
  And God called the light Day 10
and the darkness he called Night.
And the evening and the morning
were the first day.
  And God said, Let the waters
under the heaven be gathered to- 15
gether unto one place, and let the
dry land appear: and it was so.
  And God called the dry land
Earth; and the gathering together
of the waters called he Seas: and 20
God saw that it was good.
  And God said, Let the earth
bring forth grass, the herb yielding
seed, and the fruit tree yielding

fruit after his kind, whose seed 25
is in itself, upon the earth: and it
was so.
  And God made two great
lights; the greater light to rule
the day, and the lesser light to 30
rule the night: he made the stars
also.
  And God created great whales
and every living creature that moveth,
which the waters brought forth 35
abundantly, after their kind, and
every winged fowl after his kind:
and God saw that it was good.
  And God said, Let the earth
bring forth the living creature after 40
his kind, cattle, and creeping

What do these words mean: *void*; (line 4); *abundantly* (line 36); *image* (line 45); *dominion* (line 46)?
Are there any other words you do not understand? If so, find out what they mean.
Read the extract again and try to follow what happened when God made the world.

The next two poems tell the same story in much more everyday language.

thing, and beast of the earth after
his kind: and it was so.
    And God said, Let us make
man in our image, after our likeness: 45
and let them have dominion
over the fish of the sea, and
over the fowl of the air, and over
the cattle, and over all the earth,
and over every creeping thing that   50
creepeth upon the earth.
    So God created man in his
own image, in the image of God
created he him; male and female
created he them.   55
    And God saw everything that
he had made, and, behold, it was
very good.

from The Authorised Version

The Song of Creation

First He made the sun,
Then He made the moon,
Then He made opossum,
Then He made racoon.

Adam was the first man
The Lord put on the ground,
And mother Eve she was the one
Who made the good Lord frown.

All the other creatures
He made them one by one,
He stuck them on the fence to dry
As soon as they were done.

Anon.

The Creation

And God stepped out on space,
And He looked around and said:
'I'm lonely—
I'll make me a world.'

And far as the eye of God could see
Darkness covered everything,
Blacker than a hundred midnights
Down in a cypress swamp.

Then God smiled,
And the light broke,
And the darkness rolled up on one side,
And the light stood shining on the other,
And God said:'That's good!'

Then God reached out and took the light in His hands,
And God rolled the light around in His hands
Until He made the sun;
And He set that sun a-blazing in the heavens.
And the light that was left from making the sun
God gathered up in a shining ball
And flung it against the darkness,
Spangling the night with moon and stars.
Then down between
The darkness and the light
He hurled the world;
And God said: 'That's good!'

Then God Himself stepped down—
And the sun was on His right hand,
And the moon was on His left;
The stars were clustered about His head,

And the earth was under His feet.
And God walked, and where He trod
His footsteps hollowed the valleys out
And bulged the mountains up.

Then He stopped and looked and saw
That the earth was hot and barren.
So God stepped over the edge of the world
And He spat out the seven seas—
He batted His eyes, and the lightnings flashed—
He clapped His hands, and the thunders rolled—
And the waters above the earth came down,
The cooling waters came down.

Then the green grass sprouted,
And the little red flowers blossomed,
The pine tree pointed his finger to the sky,
And the oak spread out his arms,
The lakes cuddled down in the hollows of
      the ground,
And the rivers ran down to the sea;
And God smiled again,
And the rainbow appeared,
And curled itself around His shoulder.

Then God raised His arms and He waved His hand
Over the sea and over the land,
And He said: 'Bring forth! Bring forth!'
And quicker than God could drop His hand,
Fishes and fowls
And beasts and birds
Swam the rivers and the seas,
Roamed the forests and the woods,
And split the air with their wings.
And God said: 'That's good!'

Then God walked around,
And God looked around
On all that He had made.
He looked at His sun,
And He looked at His moon,
And He looked at His little stars;
He looked on His world,
With all its living things,
And God said: 'I'm lonely still.'

Then God sat down—
On the side of a hill where He could think,

By a deep, wide river He sat down;
With His head in His hands,
God thought and thought,
Till He thought: 'I'll make Me a man!'

Up from the bed of the river
God scooped the clay;
And by the bank of the river
He kneeled Him down;
And there the great God Almighty
Who lit the sun and fixed it in the sky,
Who flung the stars to the most far corner of the
    night,
Who rounded the earth in the middle of His hand;
This great God,
Like a mammy bending over her baby,
Kneeled down in the dust
Toiling over a lump of clay
Till He shaped it in His own image;

Then into it He blew the breath of life,
And man became a living soul.
Amen. Amen.

James Weldon Johnson

Which of the three versions of the Creation do
you prefer? Why?

ACTIVITY I: **Painting**

James Weldon Johnson's poem conjures up
wonderful pictures and his *Creation* would be
a marvellous thing to paint.
Split into groups. Each group take one part of
the poem to paint.
When the all the pictures are finished, join
them together to make a long "comic strip"
painting of *The Creation*.

ACTIVITY 2: **Choral Verse, Mime and Music**

The same poem also makes a very good
presentation (you could practise it and show it
to another class).
1. You would need two large groups of
   readers, *A* and *B*, to read the poem. *A* could
   read stanza one, *B* could read stanza two,
   and so on.
2. A smaller group (or one good reader) could
   read God's voice when he speaks in the
   poem.
3. Other people could mime the parts of God
   and the animals.
4. You could make up sound effects and
   percussion music to go with the
   presentation.

Biographical Notes on Poets

MICHAEL ALEXANDER (1941 –   )
Lecturer and writer who lives in Dunblane in Scotland. Likes his family, books and a quiet life. Dislikes people being cross with him when he forgets things – which happens rather a lot. Entertains his children – Lucy, Patrick and Flora – by making silly jokes and putting on funny voices.

JAMES KING ANNAND (1908 – 1993)
Annand was born and schooled in Edinburgh, and was later to teach history in a variety of his native city's schools. He was always very active in promoting the Scots tongue, as can be seen in his popular children's collections of verse – *Sing It Aince for Pleisure* (1965), *Twice for Joy* (1973) and *Thrice To Show Ye* (1979). During the Second World War, he served in the Royal Navy.

ROBERT BROWNING (1812 – 1889)
Son of wealthy parents. Had little formal schooling. Learnt love of music from his mother and love of reading from his father. Grew up to be a very successful poet. At 34 met Elizabeth Barrett, another poet. Elizabeth wasn't very strong (had received a back injury falling off her pony aged 15). Her tyrant of a father insisted on treating her as an invalid so she lay on a couch all day long. Robert married her in secret and, together with her little dog, Flush, they ran away to Italy. Elizabeth turned out to be perfectly healthy and they lived happily ever after.

ANDREW DAVIES
Lives in Warwickshire with his wife, two children, two cats (Foggy and Jemima) and a silly dog called Tanya. Writes plays, poems and novels. His novels for children – *Conrad's War* and *The Dreadful Deeds of Marmalade Atkins* – are very funny indeed.

ELEANOR FARJEON (1881 – 1965)
Born in London. Her father wrote novels and, said Eleanor, "had a way of turning such occasions as Christmas, birthdays, holidays and parties into fairy tales." Typed her own stories and poems from the age of seven.

ROY FULLER (1912 –   )
Has been a lawyer, a sailor, a Professor of Poetry and a governor of the B.B.C. Awarded the C.B.E. in 1970.

ROGER McGOUGH
A very funny writer who believes in making poetry something everyone can enjoy. Used to be a pop singer in the sixties. Appears on television and gives readings of his poetry at art festivals all over the world.

CARL SANDBURG (1878–1967)
An American poet, writer and collector and singer of folksongs. Worked as a journalist, folksinger and travelling poet. Spent thirty years writing a biography of Abraham Lincoln, one of the presidents of the U.S.A. The biography took up six volumes.

VERNON SCANNELL (1922 –   )
Has been a soldier, a teacher and a resident school poet. Now has a Civil List pension so that he doesn't have to work – except at writing his poems. Likes listening to the radio and watching boxing.

WILLIAM SHAKESPEARE (1564 – 1614)
Born in Stratford-upon-Avon, the son of a glover. After a very ordinary education went to London and became the greatest playwright and poet of his time (perhaps of any time). Acted in his own plays. Returned to Stratford in later life, built a big house and died there on his 52nd birthday. Married, at 18, to Anne Hathaway. Had three children: Susannah and twins, Judith and Hamnet.

ROBERT LOUIS STEVENSON (1850 – 1894)
Born in Edinburgh, the son of a lighthouse builder. A sickly child who spent childhood in bed. Read to by his nurse and mother to pass the time. Grew up to write stories and poems himself. Travelled widely and lived for some time in the South Seas. Died there suddenly (while making mayonnaise for a salad!) and is buried on Mount Vaea, in Samoa.

Answers to riddles on pages 36 and 37

1. A tree
2. An egg
3. A cow
4. Iron

Acknowledgements

Thanks are due to the following publishers, agents and authors for permission to reprint the material indicated.

Every effort has been made to trace copyright but if any omissions have been made please let us know in order that we may put it right in the next edition.

George Allen & Unwin for 'Little Johnny's Confession' by Brian Patten from *Little Johnny's Confession*, 1957. The late J. K. Annand for permission to quote selected bairn rhymes. Reprinted by permission. Anvil Press Poetry for 'I am clad in red' by Michael Alexander. Associated Book Publishers (U.K.) Ltd. for 'Poem on Bread' by Vernon Scannell from *All Sorts of Poems* ed. Ann Thwaite; 'Tom's Bomb' by David Hornsby from *Allsorts* 6, Methuen Children's Books. Jonathan Cape Ltd. for 'First Day at School' and 'Nooligan' by Roger McGough from *In the Glassroom*; 'Whatif', 'The Meehoo with an Exactlywatt', 'Little Abigail and the Beautiful Pony' and 'Bear in There' by Shel Silverstein from *A Light in the Attic*, Shel Silverstein. Andrew Davies for 'Supermarket Serpent'. Abdre Deutsch for 'The Longest Journey in the World' by Michael Rosen from *You Can't Catch Me*. Gerald Duckworth & Co. Ltd. for 'The Dodo' by Hilaire Belloc from *Complete Verse*. Faber and Faber Publishers for 'Night Mail' by W. H. Auden from *Collected Poems*. Harcourt Brace Jovanovich, Inc. for 'Arithmetic' and 'Buffalo Dusk' by Carl Sandburg; renewed 1978 by Margaret Sandburg, Helga Sandburg and Janet Sandburg. Reprinted by permission. William Heinemann Ltd. for 'Jargon' by James Reeves from *Ragged Robin*. David Higham Associates Ltd. for 'Argus and Ulysses' by Eleanor Farjeon from *Children's Bells*, O.U.P. Macmillan for 'To See the Rabbit' by Alan Brownjohn from *The Railings*. Leslie Norris for 'Choosing a Friend'. Oxford University Press for 'Out of School' by Hal Summers. Reprinted from *Tomorrow Is My Love*, Hal Summers © 1978 by permission. Viking Penguin Inc. for 'The Creation' from *God's Trombones* by James Weldon Johnson. We are grateful to the following for assistance in providing photographs: Popperfoto p. 21; J. Allan Cash pp. 28, 39, 40 & 41; Australian News and Information Bureau p. 29; Haags Gemeentemuseum, The Hague p. 36; BBC Hulton Picture Library p. 42; Mansell Collection p. 45.